Rainbows and Rollercoasters

Maryanne Sanders

Rainbows and Rollercoasters

For Rob, Addy, Matt and Nerissa

Rainbows and Rollercoasters
ISBN 978 1 76109 357 9
Copyright © text Maryanne Sanders 2022
Cover photo: Maryanne Sanders
Internal illustrations: Shu-Han Lin

First published 2022 by
GINNINDERRA PRESS
PO Box 3461 Port Adelaide 5015
www.ginninderrapress.com.au

Contents

Tongan whale adventure	9
Spider	11
New York	13
Norwegian Sea Eagle	15
Mother India	17
Refugee Child	19
Munch's Scream	23
Children	25
Ancient Mother	27
If only	31
Loneliness	32
What if?	33
Cyber bird mind	35
Reflections on an imminent death	36
Cult of Perfection	39
Double X	41
Happiness	45
Life is like a boat	47
Worry swag	49
Rollercoaster	51
Place	53
False friend	54
Getting it all together	55
Peace of Mind	57
No choice	58
Praise be to all good men and true	60
Operatic musings	63
Homage to my fridge	65
Time	66
Autumn	67

Winter	69
Your garden	71
Praise be to all life	72
Baby	74
Kindergym	76
Short life	77
Sprite Child	79
Wendy's lament	80
Child	82
Peacock house	83
Forever House	85
What is a gingernut?	89
Home	91
My dear life partner	93
Brevity	95
Wonderland	96
Mothers All	97
My mother tells me	100
Long love	101
My 70th year	102
My Beloved	105
Totem Pole	107
Bivalve Shell	109
And this changed my life	111
Fix it	113
Sleep	114
Prayer	115
Dear Soul	117
Homeward Dove	118
That day	119
Time Passes By	121
I know	123

Grief	124
Friends	125
Rainbow	127
Listen	128
One Day	129
Forever Days	131

Tongan whale adventure

Brave voice shouted
'Go grab your chance
Swim with whales
An opportunity there
Once in a lifetime'

Worry voice stirred up
And wouldn't stop
'You're not insured
For adventure sports
You haven't swum
Since summer
It could be
Dangerous
Unethical
Can you swim that far?
What if?
You may disappear
In that vast Pacific Ocean
Never to be seen again'

'Shut up all of you'
My hands clapped over my ears
I donned my wetsuit
Snorkel and fins
And swam out
To be with
A mummy and calf
Those wonders of the deep

Spider

It was on an Adelaide bus where I sat unaware
That a sneaky spider had hopped aboard minus a fare
Hidden in my trouser leg, not easy to swat
It climbed up, then bit; it hurt a lot

A welt swollen, red which grew and grew
That toxic spider venom – what a brew!
Two doctors, mad itching then one week on
All calmed down, the wound was gone

I live in a strange wilful country
A reckless fickle land
Where a bus spider bit me
A shock, you'll understand

The bite lasted a week, red and raw
Australian style; insect law!
I forgive that that sneaky spider, one I didn't even see
Despite all, this wide brown land is for me

New York

Some say you're a tinsel lady
Your lights are beacons
To eager aspirants flocking
Like moths to the flame
Lured by promises
Of Broadway fame
And international dazzle

But for so many from afar
You are a city of opportunity
Your welcome enfolds many
From different countries
Embracing over six hundred languages
And multiple nationalities

At Battery Park the statue
Migrant arms outstretched
Shows the fears, the hopes
Of the novitiates
Their desires and dreams

A taxi driver from Burkina Faso told me
In this city you can eat pork, beef anything
Work, and be someone

Norwegian Sea Eagle

Feathered courtship
Whirling earthwards in tandem
Talons locked
Aerial cartwheels defying gravity
Then soaring upwards
Gliding, hovering
A pair bonded for life
Home an eyrie
High on a coastal cliff

Mother India

First of all I thought this is Indian business, not my business. Then I thought again as the brutality hit home. After all, we share a global humanity at this point in history. This girl could have been any female – our sister, our daughter, anyone.

Her name means light
A luminescence lit up
Her parents' world
Radiance emanating
From the spark of her being

She showed promise
Motivated, able, her wish was
To be educated, to spread her light
One day to set up medical facilities in poor areas
Her parents supported her plans
Selling their ancestral land for her education
Not for her wedding dowry

Mother India where were you
When that bus full of evil men
Seized this child and her friend?
Fired up with alcohol, injustice and hate
They tried to extinguish the light
Using her body as a battering ram

Mother India where were you
When this child cried out for help?
An innocent, her crime to be female
In a country where some say women are flowers
But flowers are equally exquisite and dispensable

Mother India, you failed your child
Allowing the forces of evil and darkness
Sanctioned by wicked chauvinistic entitlement to
Ravage that child – everyone's child
That night in Delhi

Mother India let the light of this child
Jyoti Singh Pandey shine on
A beacon for others
Let the flame of this brave one and her family
Burn on in the hearts of our daughters and sons
So they can know good from bad
Striving so all can be equal

Refugee Child

This poem was inspired by the significant event. It was a candlelight vigil held at Rymill Park, Adelaide, on Saturday 12 July 2014 to mourn the children being held in detention at that time by the Australian government. A candle was placed on the water's edge of the lake for each child. Many there were shocked at how many candles there were.

'So sorry I am Layla, a refugee girl
Suffering in this adult tumult
When other children
Can have a home, security and peace'

'So sorry I am one of the children
In indefinite detention
Surrounded by sadness and fear
My childhood stripped to a core of trauma'

'So sorry we made for your Australian shores
The desperate escape to anywhere
Fleeing bloody oppression
Fearful for our lives'

'So sorry we bothered your navy
To enforce the policy "Stop the boats"
To be turned away, taken
To an isolated island'

'So sorry this issue has divided your country
A policy that has us dehumanised
Illegal queue jumpers who ignore the rules
But where is this orderly queue for me?'

'With death shrieks in our ears
We were forced to flee the familiar
Not because we wanted to
But through peril for our very lives'

'So sorry our hope is shattered
A no-man's-land homeless and bleak
Distraught my parents weep for all they have lost
And despair for an unknown future'

Munch's Scream

The Scream by the artist Edvard Munch is one of the most widely recognised paintings in the world. Oslo was Munch's home city. The biographical information I learnt from an exhibition of Munch held at the Oslo Art Gallery, June 2013, inspired this poem.

Life was never a warm bask in the sun
Tuberculosis – the grim reaper of my time
Took my mother when I was only five
Then my favourite sister in my teens.
Life became a cheerless universe

Those hostile mowers, sickness and death
Slayed what I loved

That day neurons converged in a frenzy of hopelessness
Jangled nerves shouted into my head
I ran to the bridge to stop those thoughts or jump to oblivion
My hands tried to stop the din
But there was no escape

My bones dissolved into formless flesh
An agony of shrieking emotions

My head became *The Scream*

Children

We are the children born of love
Cared for, wanted
Our homes a cocoon of care
And peace

We are the children who dream
Of a future wadded with
Plans and entitlements
And sweet anticipation

We are the children born of hardship
Our houses rocking with difficulty
Oaths, conflict fraught
Getting by is our mission

We are the fearful children
Who worry doing the wrong thing
Could ignite emotional tinder to
Violent conflagration

We are the children who feel less than
Our classmates who we see
Have lunch boxes packed with care
Clean clothes, nice shoes, concern

We are the children from the other side
Difficulties our companions
Our hearts darkened
By daily struggle

We are all the adults of tomorrow
Our childhoods
The society
Of the future

Ancient Mother

This poem was inspired by the book *Talking to my country* by the Australian journalist Stan Grant. This book gave me insights into Aboriginal culture and values.

Take me to your heartlands
Show me your desert plains
Star studded black night
Clear blue skies arching canopies over
Ghost gums trunked eerily white
In gorges with hidden springs
Where kookaburras laugh
And time bears witness

Your lands cradled civilisations
Was it 40,000 years or longer?
People who lived in harmony with you
Moving with the seasons
Taking what was needed
Your lands providing
Sustenance and kinship
Recorded in rock art history

For indigenous peoples
Shared land was their home
Their identity, a belonging
Forged from rocks, mountains
Water holes, familiar trees
History of where food was
Familial knowledge mapped
In primaeval storylines

Just over 200 short years ago
A moment ago in your ancient narrative
When the first whites
Saw an empty land
Their eyes glinting with expectation
Far from European constraints
Here was Terra Nullius
A land there for the taking

Some whites reaped
What they did not sow
They usurped, filched
Overturning the ancient peoples
Who cared for this land
Disenfranchising, possessing
Leaving some shipwrecks to flounder
In a sea of white fella poison

Ancient Mother
Embrace the shared dreaming
On your soils where
So many come from other lands
Nurture your primordial children
Precious genes tracing an ancient history
Embrace the shared dreaming
In this, our age-old home

If only

If only my life
Could float high
Like cloud floss
In an azure sky

If only my life
Could dissolve black mists
Of negativity
disperse them to clarity

If only my carefree
Freedom spirit could soar
In the thermals
Of eternal joy

Loneliness

I too have walked the roads of loneliness
Locked in a head that
Looks out at a world
Of purpose, fun laughter
The connexion of family groups
Solitary me, excluded

I too have walked the streets of London
Lost in a sea of millions
Going about their business
Returned to my lone bed
in a mental cave
Wondering 'What next?'

What if?

I might have
I could have
I would have
I should have
If only

Conjectures chewing up the brain
Causing angst, causing strain
So hard to focus on what is now
Always gnawing on the which and how

Meanwhile life rattles along
Rumination a wasteful song
Love for today, live the moment now, here
Or life may just zoom past, I fear

Cyber bird mind

Flitting like a bird in a forest
Darting from branch to branch
The email opens up with a weblink
I wanted to read mail
Now I am on a webpage
Distracted

A mind with no focus
Casing a plethora of leads
Going here, there
Cheeping at nothing
An empty mind
Full of expectation

Facebook, email, twitter
Cyber pathways
Often leading into the woods
Of nowhere

Once long ago I lived in country New Zealand
My mind was open, receptive
Spacious like the sky

Where will this bird mind take me?
What will it do to my time?
My satisfaction
Sense of meaning

Will this bird mind ever come to roost
In restful contemplation?

Reflections on an imminent death

Dancing body
Swirling, lost
Swaying, moving
In musical sequences
Shimmering woman
Curved, solid
Who walked
Talked, planned
Dreamt as we do
Your life frolic curtailed
By cruel fate
Which programmed your cells
From way back
Your stage now a hospice bed
With yellow flesh mouldering
A body gone awry
Pumped up with bodily fluids
With nowhere to go
Call this a gentle death?
I don't believe you
Labouring breath by breath
Mouldering flesh
Slowly dissolving
Cell by cell
Now I know this body
Is not you
Just your worldly apparel
A corporeal garb

You are still here
In this unresponsive flesh
Spirit gritted
Soon you will float onward
Where you will be free
From this dross
To soar in the thermals
And dance
Once again

Cult of Perfection

Cooing you peered into my pram
Faces full of love, smiles, care
I was a newborn baby
I was perfect

At primary school I started to learn
We are all different
Some bigger, some dumber than others
Less than perfect

With self-control I could be slimmer
Little bread, no treats, fewer potatoes
Yes there was hunger here and there
But I could move towards my ideal

By high school anorexia was my companion
Not too serious this chum
Just a come and go friend
Who guided me to perfection

Mirrors told me my breasts were too small
My butt too big
My nose too long
I begged my mother to see a cosmetic surgeon

To look better on Facebook
I needed some readjustments
The surgeon was complicit in this
'We'll see what we can do'

After schooldays there was more
Teeth whitening, dermal fillers and botox
Vaginal reconstruction, even anal bleaching
My list went on and on

Tattoos and piercings gave me that individual stamp
Like depictions on a blank canvas
An artistic sheath
For others to view my perfection

My tatt. a long-necked swan
Splayed the length of my back
Symbol of me, once an ugly duckling
Metamorphosed to beauty

Now older, content in myself
I see the lies that shaped my thoughts
I blow apart that myth of ever being perfect
Now content to be me

Double X

A random start at conception
A double X chromosome
Signals a female sexual identity
With inbuilt psychological flux

When I was a child of twelve
Those periods came with monthly blood
Pads, spills, vigilance down under
Hormonal ups and downs

Too young for that
So much else in transition
But a universal truth
Like night and day

Then the big tumult
A chosen man, trust, pregnancy
Those examinations, more down under
Then the big event

A planned Le Boyer birth
Soft lights, a warm bath music
Turned to a medical drama
After twenty four hours of trying

A happy result
A dear baby boy
But a mother tired by it all
Who had to pretend all was well

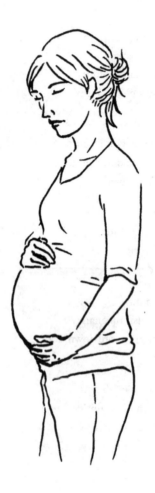

Such is the lot of a woman
Cyclical ups and downs
A rollercoaster of
Physiological change

Somehow we are the stronger sex
Our trials harden us
To the frailties
Of our mortal state

Happiness

You wipe away the tears
Bring back the dreams
Nourish the soul
And hearten the psyche

I wish I could bottle you up
Dish you out to all who grieve
Suffer, churning souls whose
Daily lives are trials

I wish I could hand you out
To ease the pain of those
Whose smiles are lost
Whose hope is dry

But you are whimsical
You come but often do not stay
You flit and offer a taste
Of joy then you are gone

Life is like a boat

I was a young girl
Floating like a boat on an empty ocean
With no anchor
Innocent of the wiles of the sea

Far from a home, alone in a big city
A port that had long ceased to provide succour
Adrift on that sea of emptiness
Longing for a place of refuge

Young man you came
With your dark looks, your exotic allure
You said you loved; I gave it all
My body, my heart, my soul

Addicted to you
Addicted to love
Surrendering my self
My power was lost

You became my controller
Mesmerised by the voice, the body
Subdued by your power
You steered my course

My boat of life
Crashed in this storm of love
Up and down the waves
Tumultuous in the chaos

Young man you lied your intent
You left, you broke my heart
Bereft aching with loneliness
I no longer trusted

You left a wreck
The boat I sailed in
Had lurched, overturned
Then sunk

I had to rebuild my boat of life
Much sturdier to be made of tougher stuff
It took a long time
But now my course is my own

Worry swag

I packed up my swag of worry
Layer of thought upon thought
Often suffocating reason
Stifling the cool oblivion of sleep
Explosively igniting
my night brain
Sleep – no way!
I packed up my worries
In that swag
I headed out from the city
From the metropolitan world
Of shopping malls and screens
And went on the road
That wends through hills
And endless corners.
On and on
To nowhere in particular
Down a bank I found
A mossy verge
And dumped my heavy swag
It fell with a thump
I headed back to the city
Much lighter.

Rollercoaster

Did I ask you to seize me
Take me on this tumultuous ride
No fun journey
Blanched, nerves taut, butterfly stomach
I hold on just
Up down I whirl along
Slave to this manic machine

Just when I thought things had levelled
A peaceful respite
I was on board the coaster again
Plummeting at speed, up and down slopes
Looping the loop
In never ending laps

This life is no sideshow
Requiring guts and strength
To hang on, not to leap off
Somehow I know that
As crazy as this ride is
If I can be brave and strong
The level will return

Place

They say
You need to live in a place
A long time
To be part of it
But I say
Home is in your heart

They say
Connections depend on place of birth
School study work
All this can help
But I say
Home is in your heart

Drift of global nomads
Impelled by love adventure work and war
Peripatetic army in motion
Some say they have lost their home
But I say
Home is in your heart

False friend

False friend
Luring and seductive
Promising you'd fill
The empty pit
In my stomach

Crooning in my ear
'All will be well'
Your liquor
Like nectar
Cheering my spirits
Spooning and dumping
My worries

Nightly you came
Aiding and abetting
Desensitising

Acid thoughts came
Weaponed tongue
Poisoning my psyche

False friend
I've had you
Take your leave

Getting it all together

Life should get simpler as the years roll on
Registered with hair turning grey
And other signs
Of age creeping in
Not all at once
But insidiously mounting
In a pile
Of telltale signs that
Things are not as they were before
They shout 'Life is finite, silly'
It's lined on my face
Blotched on my skin

But still the bills pile in
Tax returns need to be done
Go online, do this that everything
Not a person to talk to
But machines with frustrating
Commands that vary
On line bill pay add new payee
The medical tests conglomerate
There's NBN, new phones
Shiny screens with facial recognition
How can I ever get it all together?
Maybe never

Peace of Mind

May I be a salve to the anxious, the depressed
Those worried and downtrodden
Whose thoughts churn on day and night
Night and day
Pressing out optimism
Hope and happiness
Corralling thought
In a psychic prison

Like a cooling breeze let me come in
Hear me, I'm the rustle of leaves
Softly with gentle touch
I can release your chains
Free you from your prison
Take you out to the light then
Let me soothe your hot brow
And cool you in
The meadows of calm and peace

No choice

Roll up roll up you folks over 60
Those who are off the treadmill
Of work, responsibilities, daily grind
Drop your yoga classes
Your aqua aerobics, your cappuccinos
Just when you think you had it all
Please climb onto the 'Rollercoaster of uncertainty'

You have to get onboard, It's the no choice ride
The mad roller coaster ride of ups and downs
For long life veterans, some suffering
Rickety knees, bad teeth,
Arthritis, degenerative this and that
Ominous other twinges and tweaks,
and Cancer

Who is smiling at the controls
As we soar up and down
And do mad loop the loops?
Why I know that spectre – it's death himself
He smiles his hideous grin
He does his crazy antics
Stop, start, calm then chaos
Lurching the machine to fling out casualties
Flat lifeless thud to ground
To their final fall

Take me, twirl me
Up and down
In demonic convolutions
While you screech with laughter
Do your worst
I'll cling on
Till my knuckles are white
Frozen appendages
and try to enjoy the ride

Praise be to all good men and true

To the men with dinner plate hands
Who sweat and labour on the farm
Caring for animals, fencing, fixing
Labouring, slogging through all weathers
Eyes crusted with dust
Providing the nourishment to
We city dwellers who know little of such things

To the banker marketer men
Who trip to public transport
Earphones in, black brief case in hand
Cappuccino machine kitchen
Why bother with appliances?
When you can get Uber Eats, or Menu Log
Or yummy brunches overlooking the ocean?
Let's hope you can share your money spoils
For the good of all
And know that money doesn't grow on trees

To the carpenters and builders
Who scaffold to heights
Hammering, carrying, bending
Calling on strong backs and strengths
Most of us don't have
You build our shelter, our homes

To the lovers with silky skin
Who cradle our bodies
In the dead of night
And we feel the joy
Of skin to skin
And being cocooned
with love and and care

To the little boys
Who will grow up
May you not just kick a footy
But kick your ego into the dirt
And cook for others
And know that my human life is as precious to me
As yours is to you
And at the end of the day
Kindness and love will be what matters

Praise be to all good men and true

Operatic musings

Born in sweetness and light wandering through the meadows
Of love care, future promise of all good things
The world is your oyster I was told
And there were many innocent years of bucolic bliss on the farm
When all that seemed far off
Then out there not so friendly altogether
The sets weren't what I expected
Somewhat harsher, with precipitous falls
Perils to watch out for
Slithery snakes that whispered in my ear
Come with me, you'll be safe
The costumes, the hairstyles, the get outs
An elegant masquerade for what lay underneath
But the love was there, the chance to give all
To the one who stole my heart
And at times my power
But the price of love, so cruel like an operatic story
It's loss.

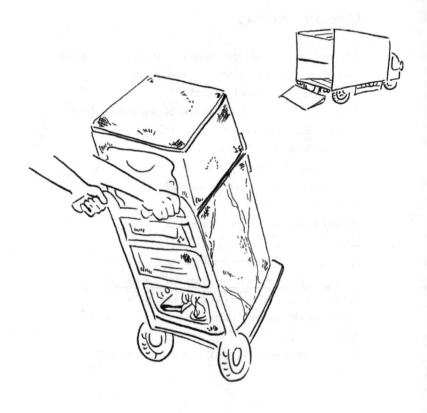

Homage to my fridge

Bless your service
Cool champion
Of forty years
Powering through hot summers
And relentless demands
Food storage reliability
And Phillips fridge cold care
Long-time giver
Venerable non-complainer

All things are transient like lightning in the sky
Your time came
Before you gave up
A Good Guys cut-price truck rolled up
The newer sleek Electrolux
Was there ready to go
You were loaded up
Rusty and leaking
At your extremities
Loaded aboard the delivery truck
Taken off to fridge heaven

Time

The long shadows of
Night turn to day
Seasons move
To a blueprint
Of predictability
Life dances to
A pattern of
Birth, ageing and death
We are a minuscule
Dot on the landscape
Of aeons of time
Why then if
Our time is so short,
So inconsequential
That this one and only life
The precious time we know
Is so precarious?
Like fragile thistledown,
Dispersed in the winds of time

Autumn

Dancing fandango
Of golden russet
Swirling sliding
Swishing
Leaves

Impending winter

Summer slides away
Gently edged out
By the early dark
Falling leaves
Colder mornings
Soon seasonal time
Will clear
The trees
Raze the foliage
And all will be
Bare

Winter

One year gone
A distant memory
Stealthily you came again
Not welcome
Uninvited

Long dark mornings
When it aches to get out of bed
Cold fingers, cold toes
Immobilised
Energy stealer

Like a blanket
Thrown on the brain
Malaise settles in
Dulling thoughts
Stilling motivation

Lucky I have my warm house
Lucky I have my warm bed
Many others are much more open
To the weather throes of wind, rain
And cold

Now you must go
You have had your time
Banish yourself, take your leave
Let the long days of
Sunshine and warmth return

Your garden

Tend it with concern
Cosset it like baby
Over time build your soil
Black and loamy
To sustain
Against the vagaries of chance
Be vigilant for pilferers
Turf out errant weeds
That choke, stifle growth
Vegetables, herbs on offer
Texture, flavour, taste
Richness for the palate
Let flowers
Flourish there
A swath of colour
Dancing floral heads in the wind
Resistant to seasonal assaults
Find your own garden
Nurture it and love it
And it will love you back

Praise be to all life

The onward upward thrust of it all
Relentlessly programmed
Growth, balance, renewal
Where did we come from?
Where do we go?

A poppy creeping from her secret dark pod
In a colourful blaze to showcase her wares
In glorious hues then retracts shrivelling to nought
The rainforest where life is born, renews, then dies
From dark shrouds ferns unfurl their green-laced fronds
Tree canopies sprout from the smallest seed.

Vegetables and fruits emerge from the soil
After solicitous plantings
With just the right nourishment, weeding and care
Apricots, persimmons, tomatoes, a bounty of food
The constant churn of old life, new life
All falls back to the dark
Then becomes soil

Infants born defenceless and tiny
In timely circuitry they emerge painfully
From the maternal vessel
Which is seized by a life force
Creating and expelling the sticky, bloody babe
Shrieking indignantly, hungrily

The mother who learns quickly that to sustain new life
There are no limits to 24/7 care
No pay raises or overtime
No starts and finishes
No nights and days

Praise be to all who love and care
To our animals, our friends, family and lovers

Like planets in the cosmos
We orbit, collide and merge
Then set off on our solitary trajectory
Once again

Baby

Baby
You are the first
First child
First grandson
First grandchild
A miracle
Chameleon
Moods changing
Happiness
To discontent
In an instant
Every flicker of a smile
A delight to
Parents on standby
You learn
Quickly
In months
To trust
A universe
Where your cries
Control your needs
Your gaze
Is pure
Steady

You grow
Every second
From that
Floppy newborn
To a child
Who can focus
And have
Interest
Baby
Miracle
You bring
Love

Kindergym

Boys and girls come out to play in leafy Burnside
An hour of gambolling and fun
On squashy mats, tunnels that lead
Under wooden structures
Babies with puzzled faces
Corkscrew hair, hair that stands on end
Toddlers climbing falling experimenting
A contained universe of texture
And curious anticipation
Fathers mothers grandparents
Smile agog at all this joy

Short life

Monody – poem lamenting a death. My dear sister passed far too young at the early age of 42 from cancer. More than ever she would have loved to be there to see her children grow up. This was not to be. Her lineage lives on in her children and six grandchildren.

You dreamt, you trusted
Your universe would unfold
Loves, job, children would come
Life events would roll out
On a long trajectory

But life was cut short

Loves became tangled jungles
Where thickets bound you in their furl
Sticky parasitic threads struck to you
You believed that you could free yourself
But life was cut short

Deep in the jungle hid a marauder
Insidious it planted malevolent seeds in your body
They grew, propagated, moved self sown
Your body could not defend; it was overwhelmed
Cancer cut your life short

Intense life, packed life
Children you longed to see grow up
Thwarted dreams, broken tomorrows

What would you have done differently
If you knew life would be cut short?

Sprite Child

A poem written to honour the free spirit of Leela Wendy. This was written when she was very young – under three. My sister would have loved to meet her six grandchildren. Leela is the first and oldest.

Sprite child flitting here and there
A curly haired babe, no worldly cares
On the lawn galloping as a horse
While often calling to mummy of course

Happy with small things, your gaze is wide
What wonderful secrets can you confide?
Plants, flowers, herbs take in your view
The shiver of leaves: each colourful hue

An infant so contented at this stage
Why does nature have to change the page?
To move along on the journey of life
With all that inherent joy and strife

Wendy's lament

You called on me, a young kiwi woman
Before I was ready; replete with life
My young family still small
My dreams unrealised
My problems unresolved

You attacked my body
Still taut, well kept and proud
The temple I had attended to with
Organic food, exercise, fresh air
You found a chink, you entered in

At first I did not take you seriously
I was too young, too strong
But you stood your ground, gaining sway
Insidiously tightening your grip
Until your siege became pervasive

Pleading, agonising I tried to bargain
You would not hear it; it meant nothing to you
Life became full of doctors, medicines and pain
Your grasp as tenacious as a parasitic plant
I could not escape

As we intermingled things changed
I had to accept you
You did not grip so hard
Our liaison was inevitable
Deep sleep would be a relief

The struggle over, you claimed me
My weary body bereft of fight was compliant

Farewell to my three children
Not ready, not willing
But summoned

Be strong my young ones
I watch over you from afar
Trusting others to do my job

See me in the wind, the moon, the stars
I am always with you

Child

You little mischievous whippet
Casting your eye around
For the action that
Has the most impact with
No regard for your safety
Or imminent danger
Grab the curtains
Wrap them around your little body
And pull and twirl till they fall
Go push the clothes stand
Till a cascade of clothes
Envelope and frighten you
The wine bottle looks interesting
Grab that, go drop it somewhere – crash!
The cords, the remote control
Fridge magnets, ornaments
Provide a cornucopia of interest
For a curious two-year-old mind

Peacock house

They 'dressed' my house
For selling purposes
Stripped it of its previous identity
Down to a blank canvas
Devoid of anything
That sniffed of labour
Or its previous occupants
Hoses, vacuum cleaners
Cleaning products
Were whisked away
Unsightly bits masked
My house and I laughed

We knew what it takes
To look after a hundred-year-old girl

Their truck rolled in
A busy team assembled
A mighty vision
Of somnolence
And pervasive calm
As seen in display homes
Beds were huge
Not just the 'Master bedroom'
Covered with multiple cushions
Throws nonchalantly strewn
With the odd book open
For leisure reading

Lounges, tables, chairs
All neutral colours
In the best harmony
Softened with faux fur

Let the new buyer
Imagine themselves
Into this vision
Of their 'forever home'

Forever House

I wave my house off
It waves back
Home for over 35 years
Californian bungalow
South Australian style
Period house
Love hate your comfort
Endless maintenance

You raised my little ones
Heard their first cries
Words, shouts, young, maturity
Watched as they edged out
Faltering at first
Then confident.
And boomeranged back
From time to time

You homed four cats
And one little Teddy dog
You cocooned us all
Protected us from all weathers
Soother, keeper of secrets
It happened within your walls

My man and I
Walked the treadmill
Of bumpy life there
Transitioning from twenty-something
To grey something else
Gritty change evolving
everyday life ups and downs
You saw it all

Goodbye house
You lift yourself up creakily
We float together aloft
Up into the thermals
Hand in hand, dreamlike
Towards forever land

What is a gingernut?

Suvla Bay, Gallipoli – a tribute to my great-grandmother, 'The NZ Gingernut lady', who cooked and distributed over four tons of biscuits to NZ troops overseas during two world wars.

What is a gingernut?
A quick crunch in the mouth
Dunking in a teacup
Anticipation of chomp and flavour

Take some flour, butter, eggs
Add a good pinch of ginger
Who could believe that so little
Could create such a tasty biscuit

Six sons left for World War One
Three fought at Gallipoli
Only four came back to New Zealand
The others war ghosts; sick, wounded

Your mother mind turned to action
You knitted for Belgian refugees
You raised funds for an ambulance in France
Troops in two world wars ate your gingernuts

The New Zealand army, navy, air force
Hospital patients and the Red Cross
All enjoyed your tins of gingernuts
The care, the effort, the flavour

Resilience is your lesson to me
Turning anxious concern to productive deeds
Away from self concern
For the good of others

I admire your get up and go
Your ability to never give up
I praise your efforts, your humanity
You gave so much to so many

In the Wellington carillon still sits the bell you brought
Titled just 'Suvla Bay'
A tribute to your soldier sons and others
Who fought on the Aegean coast of Gallipoli

Suvla Bay, Turkey; mangled bodies, bloody mayhem
So far from the land of the long white cloud
But in that gingernut kitchen, Aotearoa
A simple woman created good

Home

That barn was black
With battened door down
Still with silent nothingness
Festooned with cobwebs
Smells of old hay
and livestock manure
Stacked with
Long forgotten straw

Time stood still
There was no yesterday today or tomorrow
She was adrift
In the disconnect
No one knew she was there
No one cared

Crowds swirled past
In her head
All purpose fully striding it out
On city streets
But she was in the barn alone

Then he came looking for her
Chinks of light came under the door
Slow little rays of light
And fresh air

He came, he smiled
And she knew
She was
Home at last

My dear life partner

We give praise for our partners
Who share our journey, this finite time
We annoy each other
We confuse each other
We disagree with each other
But somehow we whirl along a tandem
Blown together by fate
We tumble around
This sweet life, this cruel life
Warming each other through winter's cold
And life's chills
As autumn leaves we coalesce, then separate
Weaving a shared history
Of people past and present, events, children
That chronology of us
which withstands the winds of time

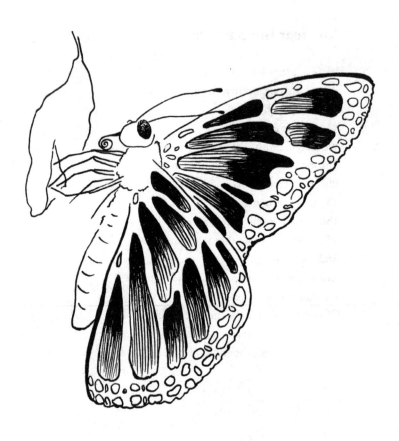

Brevity

Our brief lives pass on
Leaving fleeting footprints
All too soon
Covered by the sands of time

Apple-blossom white
Sheeted against an azure sky
Shimmering dance ephemeral

Wonderland

In memory of my artist friend David who died suddenly in NZ, January 2017. Purportedly he said, 'Take me to a wonderland' whenever he picked up his paintbrushes. His Wonderland was art.

Transport me to
A Wonderland
Where clouds billow
Over green valleys
Colour cascade of
Flowers bloom

Peace of mind
Smooth, unravelled by
War, rankling
Politics, climate change
Syrian War, Isis
Acrimonious relationships
Relentless striving

Borderless
A beauteous scape
With colourful paint
Your swirls and eddies
Can soothe my soul
Evoking freedom
Take your brush
And easel, go paint
Me to a wonderland

Mothers All

Spirit mothers whisper from afar
Of Mothers here, mothers passed
Mothers us

Praise be to all mothers
Clever women whose bodies
Created life, then brought it forth

Yummy mothers
Sipping cappuccinos ignoring distraction
Imaging dream kitchens

Caring mothers whose love
Washes over their infants
Breathing it in like air

Kind mothers whose
Soul food gives succour
To an unknowing brood

Nursing mothers whose hands
Soothe hot brows
Like cool summer breezes

Down at heels mothers
Dreaming of other lives
But rooted in their charge

Labouring tired mothers
Dragging through days
In a menial fug

Selfless mothers labouring
Night and day
In the economy of love

Lucky mothers who live
To see their children
Safely develop and grow

Praise be to all mothers
Mother mind, mother care
Mothers all

My mother tells me

Love may surface for you one day
From the deep
Your eyes beacons to your soul
Your mind his, yours his

My mother tells me
'Keep your eyes open
In this vast sea of luminous love
See the guiding lights of family friends

The eddies and flows of life
Can test a union
Swirling currents, fierce waves
Tangle of weeds, flotsam dump on shore'

My mother tells me
'Hold steady
Bolster, firm against the ocean vagaries
The strength of your supports
Securing you in the
sometimes tumult'

Long love

Decades furl we two in a mesh
Of history shared, of joys and cares
A love that intensifies
In a wake of yesterdays

Let me be there for you
Through all the turbulence of life
Support and care
Security and continuity

May I long wake up
To the curve of your shoulder
The bend of your thighs
So familiar

My 70th year

I was in my 70th year to whatever
From whatever with time to ponder
To try to make sense of all
    In my life
    It was my 70th year to whatever
When I lifted the grey Adelaide winter blanket
In the chill of trees stripped bare
    Grey gums, garden still
    Clear mind of inquiry
What will be different in a year's time?

Winds and rains blast my cold Adelaide city
Seas churn up with waves and foam
Winter sand dump, misted wave peaks
    Eddies and swirls
    All grey as death
I thought about all the change
I could see in the ocean so clearly
The wearing away of what had come before
    The sea change profound
    Of people I know
The poignancy of love and loss

I was in my 70th year to whatever
With leisure to while thought away
When I remembered farm life
    In Aotearoa
    My birthplace
A carefree explorer of rivers and rolling green
Riding my horse through gorges and farms
    Where a girl
    In the sunlight
Marvelled at the mysteries of nature

I was in my 70th year to whatever
When I thought about how it will end
I gave thanks to my special people
    The warmth of dear friends
    The care and effort
Of my long ago parents, Joline and Tom
My close family, my dear man
    Still walking life's pathway
    Hand in hand

My Beloved

When you said
I don't think I've got
Much life left in me

Tears ran like torrents
Of sadness
Waterfalls spurting
Down rainy hillsides
Like they do in
Fiordland Aotearoa

I knew then
In my heart of hearts
Your boat would move out
Soon from our shore

How can I live solitary
After decades of share?
I have to and I must

Your boat now a distant dot
Heading out to the horizon
Where sea meets sky

There's an ethereal home somewhere
Light and luminous
Freed of earthly trouble

I will join you there
In time
Arohanui
Much love
My beloved

Totem Pole

Tree in autumn of life
Mature tree limbs developed
Strong upright dominant
People looked and admired
Burnished leaves fluttering
An umbrella of green, gold and brown
But
In an instant things changed
A huge diseased limb fell
Followed by a fierce wind
Your skeleton was stripped
Leaves clumped in fallen piles
Denuded peeled back
To a skeletal frame
You became a totem pole

Bivalve Shell

Young man I found you
In London so far away
Joined like a bivalve shell
Two halves linked tenuously
By a fragile thread clasp
We have traversed our way together

Destinies intertwined
Our beach patterned
By the stuff of life
Children, house, pets and work
We have navigated our way
In turbulent and still waters
Now we have lived and loved
Forty years plus together
Years have rolled on like breakers
Shifting sands residual
Sifting grains, unsteady shore

It's late in the day; skies are grey
An ocean crashes breakers
With impending force
One of these loud swells
Will surely suck the other back to
Ocean essence; the nadir of life
When Where How?

Stripped to half in an instant
How will a bivalve be
Pared to the elements
Exposed on the shore?

And this changed my life

What happens
When a cough comes
Like a chihuahua
Peevishly yapping at your heels
'Get lost cough'
But it won't go

What happens
When the little cough
Becomes a relentless
Barking through
Night and day
Day and night
From the ground to the tree tops
So loud in the leaved canopies there
That the birds go to flight
Screeching with fear

What happens
When the doctors
Break their sinister news
And your heart
Sinks like a stone
Imaging what is ahead
And how could I ever live without you?

What happens
While I call your name
And know that life will never be the same
That this cough
Could subsume
The cool ingress and egress
Of your breath, of life
And leave my landscape parched and bare

What happens
When you learn
That life and death
Are not as divisible as you thought
And one easily melds into the other

Fix it

The years roll on
Like clouds in a busy sky
Our history becomes a climate
Of yesterdays
Picture perfect days, storms
And all in between

Your eyes
Shop worn and tired
From the vagaries of precarious health
Stare deeply into my soul
They say 'Fix it'
Oh that I could wave my magic
Instant renewal

Meanwhile you are not alone
Let me be your weather vane
Read the winds
Take you to a quiet glade
Where we can lie on our backs
And watch the skies
In calm

Sleep

You too changed
Along with everything else
You used to be that black blanket
That cocooned my body from dark to dusk
Then slowly, imperceptibly
You became diaphanous
A theatre of thought
With gauzy curtains
Where black scrolled
To abrupt wake ups
To thoughts
Scrolled to past ruminations
To future ponderings
Then black respite

Prayer

Let me hang in when the going is tough
Ride the waves, the tumult, the despair
My surfboard rides the big seas
So little calm, so little respite

Tow me out to beyond the big breakers
Let me be free in that world
Of the still endless ocean
Reaching out to the horizon

Take me beyond the churn
The egg-beater whirls and eddies
Of the white caps
Swirling close to shore

Dear Soul

If walls could speak
They'd say they have seen
How you were
Gathered up here
Cosily cocooned
Your soul soothed
Your body calmed
Your brows stroked

If walls could speak
They'd say to
That worn body
Racked with cough
Tremulous breath
It's all right: it's okay

If walls could speak
They'd say we'll move
You with love and care
From this home
To the next
Like a bird
Flying off into
The sunset
To its nest

Homeward Dove

Let me be your feathered guide
My heart heavy with care
Winging it through the clouds
Of anxiety, the storms of panic
Through the discomfort,
The maybes and what ifs of
A future that is not a future

We snug together
Nestled in cosy comfort
Time comes; I'll fly
You safely upward
And onward
To your new home

That day

The day we laid your sick body to rest
The birds rose as usual
Night merged into day
Chasing away the ominous
Sick rumblings of the solitary dark
When there was just you and me
And a lot happening

The day we laid your body to rest
We knew what we had to do
My dear daughter and me
Too long, too hard
It was your time
Time to be free
Time for your wings

The day we laid your body to rest
The tumult that was your sickness
Started to evaporate
And vaporise into the ether
Of the universal cosmos
Where spirits soar and are free

Time Passes By

After my best friend and long-term partner passed, I had a crash course in the brevity of life and how things can change in an instant. I can hear him saying to me, 'Keep moving, girl, don't waste time.' This poem is written in response to that.

I never really thought about you
In those wayback days
My young time in Aotearoa
Endless summers rolled past
Grasses redolent with cricket noises
Chamomile knee high
Where a girl spent vacuous hours
Lying on her back
Fluffy cloud gazing
And dreaming of far away places

Often I tossed you in the air
Juggled and twirled you around
You stretched yet stayed

Riding my horse along the Mangaone riverside
Your signature was there
Etched in the rocks, the carvings of the river shape
The trees, some ancient hills
Landscape was your canvas
But I didn't see it back then

Further down the track I took notice
Where once you were a kaleidoscope to the future
You became a concertina to now
Compressed and spent

'Don't waste me,' you whisper
Don't waste TIME.'

I know

I know now that 40 years of companionship
Can be taken in an instant
Like a tree trunk floating down a swollen river
Our shared history carried on the currents
Churning in the eddies and swirls of water

I watch but cannot snatch back that which has gone
Left with the museum of a life shared
Clothes like statues in an unused wardrobe
The imprint of his sleeping shape on the bed
The empty chair, the echo of quiet and still
Shared memory gone, only my head carries it.

Precious time, dear companion
I bless the decades we spent
In homely togetherness
Our ups and downs
Tiffs and reconciliations
A mature and comfortable
Equanimity now

I know now that we two were at home with each other
For so long so long
Now he must float in my memory
His face, his voice
Resurrected from deep in my mind

What shall I do, what shall I do?

Grief

Let me tell you how grief is
Like rain, soft drizzle pitter pat
Gentle background soundscape
As unobtrusive as thistledown in a wind
But storm menace can blow up in an instant
Pelting down splats of water
Gulping, I struggle to breathe

While remembering him
And what happened
Think too long and a tumult of thought deluges
Forming a maelstrom of turbulence
That bend all in its path

Then skies clear and all is okay again

Friends

Our friends, our precious friends
Like autumn leaves we are blown together
Bared from our mother trees
Alone, tremulous, we tumble along
At the will of errant gusts of wind
Meeting others, building up, stripping away
Twisting, turning, making pirouettes
Sometimes gyrating in mad circles
Together, apart, solitary, grouped
Hanging in there
Just

This world, this one and only life
Such happy times, such sadness, such despair

Praise be to our cherished companions; our dear friends

Rainbow

Let's rejoice in this rainbow life
A thing of beauty which disappears
Into the aeons of time
Soon after coming into existence

Let's rejoice in the onward upward thrust
Of new grass springing everywhere
Born again from droughts
And hard weather times

Let's rejoice in the Sophia tree
Disfigured in the freak mini tornado
Amputating huge limbs in an instant
Now dressed in a lush green canopy yet again

Let's rejoice in new life, old people, new people
Babies limp and helpless
Whimpering for succour and support
They grow up and the cycle of life starts again

Let's rejoice in the persistence of life
Its resilience and sad transience

Listen

Let my words be like cool drizzle
That seep into your mind
Not like big fat raindrops
You try to catch
In the cup of your hand
And make your own

Listen to my words, their drizzle
Can softly rain upon you
Water etching patterns in your mind
Observe, listen, reflect
To the rain of my words
Be my listener, companion, friend.

One Day

One day this walkin' talkin' body
Gonna say enough is enough
Gonna mosey out the door
Never to come back
Gonna say 'So long house'
No more leaky taps, no more bills

Gonna drop off this heavy garb
Thank it for the job its done
No more toenails to cut
Or Mammograms

Off to a different place
Where there's lots of folks I know
My long ago mother and father
My friends; family in sweet spirit world
And Freedom

Forever Days

Sing me a song little bird
A song of halcyon days

Azure shimmering water on a quiet beach
Lines of white caps in a procession to shore
The whoosh of water, sun and sand

Carefree summer; ice cream days
On such a day our family cocoon
Nested on grainy sand
That day when Vegemite sandwiches never tasted better
Our children with busy intent
Built water tunnels around sand castles
Until they became moats

She looked out to the blue horizon
She looked at him
He gazed at her
And all was sweet and lovely

Sing little bird
Of times that felt they'd go on forever

But they didn't

CPSIA information can be obtained
at www.ICGtesting.com
Printed in the USA
LVHW011317040822
725122LV00011B/323